By

Susana Peña

Life evolves into Love

Life evolves into love

Publisher
D'har Services
P.O. Box 290
Yelm, WA 98597
www.dharservices.com
info@dharservices.com
dharservices@gmail.com

Cover by Xiomara García
Cover photo by Angel
Copyright© 2016 Susana Peña

ISBN-13: 978-1-939948-41-0

All rights reserved.
No part of this book may be reproduced in any form or by any means, including photographic, photocopying, or electronic process or in the form of a phonographic recording; nor may it be stored in a retrieval system, transmitted, or otherwise be copied for public or private use-other than for "fair use" as brief quotations embodied in articles and reviews, without permission in written from the owned author.
The author sent us his own writing corrections.

ÍNDICE

This day is holy 07

The fruits of Eden 09

Exodus 12

The dust 14

The immutable genes 17

The monastery of Saint John .. 19

Do we need a compass? 21

Those stormy seas 24

The music of Beethoven 27

The northern lights 30

Les mots de dieu 33

Lady psychology 34

Stem cells are calling 37

The quest for happiness 39

A hidden girl 43

From the mountain top 47

"In the beginning... 51

The irruption of Jesus 52

"...As I have told you" 55

Dancing to paradise 56

The lady with so many names. 59

The closet 61

Spirituality vs. reality 63

References: 67

THIS DAY IS HOLY

Introduction

I have two names for this attempt to be a book that gets to your heart. One is Angels in the Roof, yeah! Though nobody sees them they be moving things around. The other is Life evolves into Love. You have to read it to see if it is true.

Live Laugh Love

This says a sign in a Doctor's office. It is a sum of the new postulates within the new positive psychology. I, of course, fully agree with it. The problem is that it is not easy, especially in moments of frustration and duress. This does not intend to be a fix all problems, nor a how to do book, less, one to try to obtain the luminous sign above.

I just pretend to review superficially, as elusive it would be otherwise, the creation with its extraordinary facets and marvels that can spring from living face to face with reality and with a sense of spirituality. If I would only obtain a glimpse of those grandiosities that surround us I'd be more than happy.

A note: I do use common words and I use contractions accepted by our Grammar. All along I like to be simple, quoting people of great knowledge in the different areas as to avail my readers of a more vital sense on the comprehension for which I avowed myself to it.

THE FRUITS OF EDEN

The trees of goodness and of badness.

There are people that miss the good in life for fear of the bad.

I think about the famous couple, what if they had not eaten of that fruit, we wouldn't have the chance to struggle as we have to make things happen, as they all were given. I am not making light of that event that set things up for real, but think about it, if we didn't need to work to get the things we need, we would be looking around with a different tune. Yes. We would have missed the opportunity to have a time in the world, but we have had the great chance all the time to elect, to pick, to battle, even to switch from bad to good, then, should we thank Eve, even the serpent?

Why the apple? Not Apple 5 or 6. It is beautiful, no doubts about it, but why the apple was chosen? Because it keeps the doctor away? It is a solid fruit, inviting, lads use them in sketches for inciting girls. Why life is like that? Should we ask, instead of why the apple, why it is a perennial temptation not to do good but to do what it pleases. Yes, we hear, go ahead and do it, that's what life is about. Too many questions for such a hearty topic, Eden, it kept reveries in our hearts.

Back to the fruits as a symbol.

We are not able to forget that fruits have a time, the timing of things. We find it in the book of Wisdom, a time to be born, a time to laugh, a time to be sad, a time for everything, I like some interpretations that say: but the best of times is the one we spend talking with the Lord. Ask Him, then, why the apple. Is He going to tell us, that it is a symbol, that the real reason is the tree of Knowledge, reserved for God, not for men? But they wanted to be like God. But they weren't. Thus, they crashed on a hard earth and took us along the way. Why, I quoted? You guessed it, too many good people don't believe in that story of Adam and Eve as people developed in different parts of the world, as Science almost has been able to prove. I say almost because there is always a corpuscle.

Still, the apple continues to be a symbol of temptation as well as of a healthy fruit. I would say, eat it with a grain of salt in your mind.

EXODUS

From immemorial time people have had the urge of moving looking for a brighter life. They were called nomads when the exodus was more scattered. Civilization set in somehow, the Spirit working on humans to stabilize them.

However, exodus continued in different ways with different people. We have the image of the Israelite exodus when freed from the Egyptian enslavement. There were times of more stability. Then, circumstances, let's call them that way, for not pointing fingers to figures born to dominate, born to inflict whatever pain they could in name of progress or religion.

At present moments exodus are called immigration, they are flows of people, a constant flow. Those receiving countries, realize it or not, are all shook up but there they are. At times the flow is a massive one as it is from Syrian at the time of this edition. Maybe when you read this it might be different.

The fact is that in spite of the suffering, exodus, small or big, brings commotion but they may also bring acculturation both ways. The recipients resent it; however, they may be beneficial in many ways. Yes, even economic benefits may occur, cultural and spiritual ones as well.

Notwithstanding, they are strongly refused at times, but exodus might bring dilation of the hearts and for that they may be blessed by those Angels in the Roof.

THE DUST

The universe is full, no doubt about it, though full is not the word because it denotes completion and the universe, vast as it is, is still growing. Does it expand? Expand to where? But it is supposed to encompass everything, how could it grow? More questions than answers.

Now, celestial bodies expel dust, then, that dust sort of stays aloof. However, there is a force in the universe that promotes cohesiveness, but where does this force come from?

There is a thought process taken from no more no less than from Albert Einstein (Ref # 1) when he describes the supposed difference between the gravitational matter and the inert matter, how after all they might conclude very much alike in their process. Of course, to understand the mind and the thought process of the master physicist is nearly impossible for an ordinary person, but with much respect I dare to say, that part of this matter he is talking about has gravitated down forward and has been united to another inert matter that happens to be floating somewhere, and that is just the beginning of the great mystery of the new formations.

Therefore, that attraction from or derived from the force forms new elements, let's call them that way, and then some celestial bodies start to emerge. They might be given different names according to their shape and function.

Also, there are the galaxies with their luxurious display of magnificence, heat and light. Most of them are stars, suns, and others planetoids that revolve around some sun in their orbit. Which role the galaxies take in this involuntary formation of celestial bodies? They might imbed them paternally? How sweet!

The perennial human quest, are there other habitable worlds, similar condition as ours? I leave you with that beautiful thought, desire or fear.

THE IMMUTABLE GENES

They are not so any more, or at least, I learned it recently. People use the genes as excuses for behavior, good or bad.

In a recent study, The Interplay of Genes, (Ref # 2), it is found that genes interact with the environment, for the array of factors chasing and impinging upon them. Thus, no more excuses like it's in my genes and nothing I can do about it. Of course, some may ask, the environment, is it?

Life in a baby is taken for granted, not revealed, but from then on it is in a constant interaction between surroundings, factors create reactions, and the results are changing to a new level of complexity.

How about God's genes, Jesus had genes, He didn't procreate except in the DaVinci Codes. So, God's genes stopped there. Do not tell me that Jesus had those of Mary's ascendance, because to me those genes should have been spiritual. In fact, where to cross the line that divides matter and spirit? Ask the professor Einstein again who defined matter as energy in the last resort? Or am I reinventing his relativity theory? (Ref # 2a).

See, where this discussion has taken us, to Science, which so many a time has come across with the unexplainable ranging in the Theological realm? This mutability and interactivity seems that after all, this has the genes of the divine.

THE MONASTERY OF SAINT JOHN

In the island of Patmos, Greeks, there is a monastery. A famous one, named after the Evangelist, one of the 12 apostles, the one Jesus "loved more", as it is said, noted for appearing reclined on Jesus in the DaVinci's Last Supper painting. This monastery was built after St. John's death.

He is known for having written the Apocalypse's in a cove there, which is preserved to these days. There is a spot in the cave were St. John touched at the beginning of his daily prayers. People up to now like to introduce a finger in it in search for pardon and peace.

The monastery offers others places decorated with the more famous religious paintings and with golden threads hanging from the ceiling where they are.

This monastery was occupied for a long time by Russian Orthodox monks, around 300 hundreds of them, later on, other monks went there. It is noted that since its inception there is not one day, rain or cold, that the place hadn't had a visitor. This information was provided by Camila, (Ref # 3)

DO WE NEED A COMPASS?

In the modern world we find instructions in anything we buy. Many cars already have GPS to take us anyway we want.

If this is so in the material world, how much more it should be in the spiritual realm. Being so, we find three types of people. The first group would say: "surely we need a guide in our lives" and soon they would go to a counselor or psychologist. How about a priest or pastor? "To a pastor, to a priest?" they might say, "no, they are not open minded enough, well, some may be", and they might look around for some guidance.

Another group would say: "no, not really, we don't need a guide, we have our intelligence, our experience, and we know ourselves better". No doubt about it, we are able to conduct our lives, ourselves. That's true but, sometimes, we can be fooled too.

A third group would say, 'it depends on the type of conflict or situation in which we are. In small cases we may come up alright one way or another. But in other areas that are more complex it is more difficult". I knew a court judge who used to say "life brings about problems but she herself solves them", yes, but in what way. This seems to be the relativism that has taken over us, that in reality nothing matters as long as we don't alter our routine.

I would say that there is still a fourth group that could say, "Yes, we need some guidance, but we already have it, the best of it, Our Lord Jesus, as simple as this". It is called love, (as that inspired Spanish song of Jose Luis Perales (Ref # 4) coming from a Saint Paul's epistle many a time read at marriages), love, that describes the different aspects of love that unfortunately we often tend to forget. That, precisely, could be the needle of the compass. The one that, more often than not, gyrates towards the brother.

THOSE STORMY SEAS

Those seas....

We have read in the Gospel about the time the apostles feared a tempest in the open sea, seeing Jesus sound sleep like unaware of the coming danger.

We have images of a rough sea many a time that we feel tossed around by opposing circumstances and we have failed to see any way out successfully. The drowning sea.... We all fear drowning, it is natural, it is such a horrible way to die. It is curious that Jesus chose that situation to show a sleeping faith that is awakened by fear. He wants us to trust Him for sure, that it is repeated in real life in almost everyone at one point or another.

Rare as it may seem, abandonment is preached as a solution. I cite Saint Paul of the Cross, not one of the popular saints, but who has a metaphoric content picturing God goodness as an ocean. Yes, an ocean can be calm, a source of peace, and also an instrument for covering the abandonment, an element of love. Love, there is the abrasive love. And by pointing out to it, we see how abandonment could be a source to turn out successfully in many of our situations, small and big.

Now, let us turn to some animals of the sea that we should not forget about them. According to Delgado, (Ref # 5) sharks, the tyrants of the sea, are not as bad as they are pictured, they do attack, and we have to be advised of their presence in whatever depth we are or want to be. They do smell humans and animals' blood and there they go. They are the vacuum cleaners of the sea, but they wouldn't go near whales.

The sea is intriguing. Men don't know yet all the reaches it contains. More and more different algae, the primal organism in the creation, are sold worldwide for treatment of different ailments. No one can see it all, but everyone can try to look inside out innermost being and realize when the waves of our passions threaten to rock our delicate boats.

Life coolors into love

THE MUSIC OF BEETHOVEN

Why have I chosen this composer? Questions and more questions. What I would really like for you is to follow a road of questions and investigate them 'cause we are in this intriguing world. So, why, existing others so big classic composers as a beautiful rainbow in front of our ears I picked Ludwig Von. Beethoven, the deaf man, this in itself puts him apart. It occurs to me to compare his music to one of those sumptuous ballrooms with luxurious lamps hanging from the ceiling that we see in movies of that time with couples making their entrance, women with their long dresses, radiant necklaces, their gentlemen introduced, announcing their name using a staff. In entering, they are engaging in smooth chatting, eating little bits of delicacies and/or beginning to dance at the sound of some waltzes. Are you thinking that Beethoven didn't like waltzes? Hear the variations he made of waltzes, "Three variations on a waltz" (Ref # 6). Anyway, that's the image his music suggests to me.

The most important input is a quote from a good "connoseur", Hamilton, (Ref # 7) , who told us of a precious thought from the great Ludwig Von, saying that classic music was a mixture of the spiritual and the sensuous. The spiritual part is no surprise as classic music is like a paradigm of spirituality. But, sensual? Yes, because classic music is a reproduction of life. There might be people who may find it boring and I respect their opinion, but I believe those who think so is because they have not submerged themselves into this kind of music.

Life is a mixture of spirituality and sensuality. Don't we have senses? Ladies and gentlemen God didn't make this world from paper and ink, let's keep discovering from what he made it, and what are we going to do with it. If you still doubt it, if you have the chance, listen to the Beethoven's Sonata # 32 in C Minor and you'll hear the two main elements of life grabbing your heart in the process.

THE NORTHERN LIGHTS

Magnetics fields have always existed in the universe but maybe because we are more aware of them now we see them dominating even the earth poles. They are changing and with that the whole earth, there are occult forces we once named them at random. The whole phenomenon leads us to watch and to find ways to counteract them like with tsunamis.

In the positive side we find the Northern lights, also propelled, as some say, by magnets.

Light makes a difference, it is the guidance and thrill of the heart. Light from above directed the sailors in ancient times, the same as the travelers on the ground. How then it would be many beautiful lights all together at one point of the world? We don't have the chance to see them anywhere, any time, it has to be in the Artic pole at dawn, the phenomenon called "Aurora Borealis". Authors attribute some of that phenomenon to the magnetic fields that exist. Others explain that particles mixed with solar rays produce either the orange or the pink light sensation.

It reminds me of the first stage of the Divine Verb in Mary's womb. It is said in the Scriptures that when she went to visit to take care of her elderly cousin who was pregnant, that as soon as this one saw Mary she sensed the movement of her own child. Was there a light, a different kind of light? To me yes, one that enlightens the soul.

Do we have magnets in ourselves? I dare to say yes, and that we should use it for good, because a chain will occur and like with the lights it will delight humans, even the stars that some of them needs to recapture lights, and for sure, our God.

LES MOTS DE DIEU

Nous voulons dit le suivant:

Donnez une subventionne a tous les pauvres de la region.

Vouz pouvez compter avec notre donationnes, nous resterons tranquille que nous aurions une reponse de Dieu.

What is this, why is it here? The mind of the author, who could understand!

LADY PSYCHOLOGY

This lady tells us that we are not able to give love if we don't have it. And it is true. It translates into that you are not able to give love if you have not received it first. She also tells us that the first seven years of life are what makes us for life. Then, we need to have received love in a package of seven years, the first ones of our life. True. Now, some may say that they know people that have received lots of love in their childhood who are tremendously selfish.

First of all, how do we know if those people really received love? by the gifts, the material things received, that is not indicative of real love.

We talk about Psychology as a Science of the mind in reference to love which is a feeling; it also has to do with spirituality. We remember the second commandment of Christ, made with the same importance as the first one, that says, love your brother as you love yourself.

One thing is apparent. The child is born wanting the best for self and for the most part they know how to ask for it.

I suppose that religion exists to try that people put a limit to that self love. It is also supposed that an inordinate love of self was the first problem of humans. Women and men wanted to know it all, this the Bible says, thus, this is a different matter, but it is possible that parents and relatives can be examples that we are not alone in the world. For some reason we live in communities, that we all have the same beginning and the same end, but in the range of years there could be a great disparity.

    This is precisely the struggle, to learn real love, to leave the garbage that benefits no one. For that we have Angels on the Roof that are constantly watching us even when no one notice them and may teach us, if we listen, how to love despite anything else.

STEM CELLS ARE CALLING

One great development in medicine has been the multiuse of stem cells. It is unfortunate that it has happened at the time of increasing subsequent use of aborted parts of children.

Stem cells or Mother cells, the Spanish name, because of the way they regenerate, are open to be developed into other many types of cells. Therefore, offering the opportunity to be used at different levels of the human body. It has been proved that the rather under developed cells have the potential to regenerate tissues in different parts of the body in different organs, from the skin to the heart, to cite just two They are calling without a voice because many people are reluctant for a variety of reasons, and the industrious medical doctors who see their potential are ingeniously offering their views in popular medical magazines, newspapers and even through the radio.

The general public, unless directed by a trusted professional, doesn't know what to do. Many insurance plans do not cover those procedures depending on many facets of the situation. Disbelief occurs along with lack of knowledge. That has happened with many other human inventions. It is said that some people at the time of the invention of electricity were still using candles. So, it is not a strange phenomenon. I see it as an exact example of life evolving into love for the benefit of the sufferings. I wish their voices, those from the stem cells, it they have one, could be heard around.

THE QUEST FOR HAPPINESS

No culture has been barren from this universal quest. That it has been different? No doubt about it. Cultures mold the minds or the minds mold the quest depending on the enclave in History and Geography.

In an interesting lecture, Father Juan Jesus Lopez, (Ref # 8), attested that culture comes before language and I fully agree, and I also add, that the quest above mentioned intertwines with culture and circumstances but it is persistent as it could universally be, though as varied as individuals exist, tailored, of course, by their diversity.

One aspect I would like to touch on is the tendency, I don't doubt whether to call it necessity, this is exactly where discussion is going, to have dreams and to try to make them happen. Some people, maybe a larger number, have found themselves disillusioned when dreams are fulfilled, or at least, not in completion with themselves as they originally thought when they were working on them. However, depending on the kind of dreams, age and further development of the person, many people have found themselves in a new level of contentment, if we don't want to call it happiness, the big word.

The exactness of a raffle.

We all have watched raffles and the exactness portrayed on them in the faces of the participants. Everybody looking around expecting the winning number!!! Why do we need a raffle? Do we need it every week, every day or every hour to keep us alert? It seems so. Hum...

Now, let's talk about mulch and interpret it within the spiritual realm. Thinking about life's struggles it seems that we actually need a mulch to cover us from scratching ourselves.

I would dream of a place where this exactness exists about anything that could happen at the moment. Let's see: Faces blushes, eyes open, all wanting to see ahead of time to know what is coming, to get to know the future, the yearning for events. And at the same time, we had developed a spiritual mulch to guard us from unnecessary spiritual pollution.

Life evolves into love

A HIDDEN GIRL

Over there, for certain mysterious place, a girl by the name of Namary was seen among bushes and wood trees. Her eyes were always looking upwards, maybe to be able to make eye contact with people, probably taller than her because she used to bend herself. Her look denoted inquisitiveness, but also great pleasure of what she was seeing around her.

When she realized that she had been spotted, she usually fled, and if at the time the other person was quick and got her trying to escape Namary used to say "let me go, I am in a hurry".

Where this strange character came from? She used to wear a hat. Well, I forgot to tell that this occurred in a time when children used to wear hats. Her clothes weren't ragged, but they weren't tidy either.

No one tried to investigate where she came from. Yes, and nothing rare was detected. This girl came from an average home with two siblings, an older boy and a younger girl that seemed to need some extra care. Maybe that explained Namary's urge to explore the world.

How are the looks of a child that desires to see with a profound sight, with a keen interest in everything. This natural apprehension more or less needs some protection. In Namary we can certainly say see, the universe is within her because the universe is candid, right there, in front of us, but also hidden in the smallest things.

There is another character, Lyra, appearing in the movie The Golden Compass, (Ref # 9) a young girl trying to find a place in the world that could reconcile her aspirations and the gratifying lights she is able to see. Which one of the girls is more real, more genuine to us? Namary, represents all that we are subjected to in living. Lyra has much of a creative mind behind her, very lovely character too. Whenever we talk about young people, if they are females, more so, our imagination mixes with a grandiosity hidden in the singularity of each life.

And what about the grace of the Creator? Where do we see it keener, in the majestic or in the simplest things, in children or in the universe? I guess it depend on the eyes of the beholder or in the surrounding circumstances. But, if it were so, we would say that "flow…, (following a church song named "Shine, Jesus, Shine. Ref # 10) by Kendrick: "Send forth your Word, Lord, and let there be light". Over each individual and over the nations, and I underscore, where the song says: "shine on me, shine on me". We all need it.

FROM THE MOUNTAIN TOP

Placidly two men were coming down sharing their own philosophical views about life. The conversation focused on which attitude was better when facing problems. One of the two, named John, was saying that to worry about those mentioned problems was a loss of time as, one way or another, for good or bad, somehow the problems would be resolved.

The friend, Peter, was saying that he couldn't by any means leave things unresolved, that he would go crazy, that he needed to worry until he could develop a plan to resolve whatever it was that was preoccupying him. Thus, the two men were descending, very carefully, pausing from time to time under the shadow of a tree.

John, praised Peter's attitude, his need to resolve things even those of daily living, but he insisted that to be worried was not the best. Peter, on the other hand, praised John's tranquility to decline worries not doing anything.

The friends, then, cited examples, and came to some considerations, established their differences over the nature of the problem in question.

From time to time the discussion focused on the point of not listening to the other just to prove each other's point of view.

Right there were the friends when one lady of certain age was passing by lifting some goods she just had bought in town. The friends paused, looked at her but neither of them offered any help to the lady.

What had happened made the men realized without telling each other that in front of necessity there is no philosophy but an urge to move and to make things work.

Peter went ahead in telling John, "I think you are right, life is too complex and has too many ups and downs to worry so much ahead of time, and that it actually never helps to solve any problem". John, put his arms around Peter's shoulders, and moving his head from side to side, told Peter, "excuse me, but I don't agree with you one more time, because what do matter is to solve any problems as we may have, even when some of them can't be solved soon enough for our liking, but it bring us peace and confidence on our strength and on the future.

And the mountain, what would it say today to these men seeing the lady walking up with her load? She seems to have said, "the best way is to keep watching the sky that is being very cloudy, with the hope that the good old lady gets to her home and that you keep on going your way before 'cats and dogs' come down on you".

"IN THE BEGINNING...

there was the Verb, and the Verb was in God, and the Verb was God. He was, in the beginning, with God. For Him everything was made, without Him nothing was made of what has been made. He is life and life is the light of men. And light shines in darkness, and darkness did not receive Him". (Ref # 11). There is nothing to add.

THE IRRUPTION OF JESUS

As it had been prefigured in the Scriptures, in the prescribed time, the Verb incarnated into a woman's womb, as a Jew.

No one can really know the numerous circumstances that had to have occurred so that the Light of the World, the Flower of Life, the Verb, would make his appearance on Earth. But, the elements were there, men of all avenues were in expectance of Him even without knowing it. Some got the great privilege of meeting Him personally, others were curious, intrigued, but walked away at least at the moment, some had a deep feeling about Him, not knowing either how deep it was in their hearts. Others came close but left, others, a bunch, 12, 72, the exact number is not known, followed Him and the world started all over in a spiritual band. It is not that spirituality didn't exist. Spirituality must have existed maybe in a cocoon, since the very beginning. But it matured, feeling it, thinking, developing, as grace made its appearance more directly fashioned around minds. And the showering of the right knowing and the profound feelings that turned around everything didn't happen until that moment of explosion, the coming of Jesus. As He enfolded His teachings He began to touch lives from inside out, and we human beings began to realize that He was, that He is, God made man, the Truth, the Life, and the Way. I can only say: Alleluia a hundred times!!!

The Grace flowing from our Lord Jesus Christ had to be enough, according to one of Paul's epistles, to keep going in his life, that was so, but so much, given to the Lord, and for what he underwent so many hardships. That was said by Jesus to Paul when he was praying. If for him it was enough, ("my grace be enough for you", were Jesus' words), what would it be for us that are making all kind of mistakes at any time? More graciously, Father Juan Jesus tells us (Ref # 12): "No two lives go about the same into the Mystery of God". Surprisingly true.

"...AS I HAVE TOLD YOU"

If you were to find an emerald in the streets you probably would like to take it and try to confirm that it is real. Still, your urge to tell it to someone you trust would be right there. There is a saying that you can be sad alone but that if you are happy you are not going to really be glad until you share it with someone, with the right person, I would add. This is the basis for needing to share the good news of Jesus. You wouldn't even need someone to prompt you, just ourselves suffice.

DANCING TO PARADISE

For some people Jesus did not look right for having been found in some festivities, it is said, in Cana's weddings. At that time there were weddings that lasted days, and, for what it seems, people enjoyed them much.

Dancing is old as people. At any time and with any rhythms humans have moved their body in compliance with their rituals and ideas. As civilization evolved dances were more sophisticated, as the adagio says, but with another intention, 'they danced to a different tune'.

Model of sophistication is the ballet. In this rigorous type of dance their apprentices are subjected to hours of practice. From there famous ballerinas with their "partenaires" have been known around the world. Other types of dances have made their appearances as numerous as the human invention can make.

Chopin's etudes # 22 and 23 seem to be telling us something. By the way, I say, music is not an invention of men even though it takes each composer's name. In # 22, it seems like pounding, we might try to put steps into and there is no way. In # 23, it is more romantic, that chanting in the middle of many notes up and down, (Chopin was a master on that). We are trying to make some meaning of dancing and I am taking it from piano pieces which don't allow dancing but allow majesty, and that is what it is going to be. Who will remember then the troubles he/she went through doing this or the other, as it is written that the woman forgets her pains after the child is born. And, I add # 24, because that is the coming, the entering, the surprise, something like St. Paul had a chance to view, yes, with capital, THAT, and we won't know where to turn, we would be surrounded from top to bottom, amazed as we have never been, but at the same time looking for someone known, Jesus trying to embrace us, and we trying to dance so as to release our appalled mind. I repeat the title, dancing to paradise.

THE LADY WITH SO MANY NAMES

From ancient times some prophets had announced that a Virgin will give birth to a child. I will not go into this, it is a great mystery of the many that surrounds us, but I would like to point out how a Jewish young lady had been chosen to be the mother of Jesus Christ. It is important to recognize that Jesus was born from a woman not form a leg or arm. Thus, what this means is the whole motherhood at its best as it is natural in the Hebrew people.

What I want to emphasize is that most people find maternity as great, as a symbol of love and dedication, so that we are not aggrandizing the role of Mary into the salvation history. That by honoring Mary we are not creating some kind of feminine deity. Mary's motherhood is in the Scriptures and it is also imbedded in our hearts. Strange, then, would be that she has so many names, rather, last names?

THE CLOSET

There is a segment of Scriptures where it talks about a man, I guess he is old, who brings up the new and the old to explain things. Thus, anybody could imagine the title here as a similar phenomenon, that I might be able to bring anything and everything from my closet to prove any point. No, the closet is what a guy, named Axel, (Ref # 13), labels that way, it is my car.

There is not a spot where something is not laying on, leaving my passengers in a quandary of where to sit, where to put things, nicely? You would expect that, but, my cherished things are thrown at times, depending on the mood of such 'passengers', how many sit at one time, or a combination of the factors. Still, the 'cotidienne', (added French for sophistication of this rather homely chapter), riding around with their 'baggage'. Many quotations meaning whatever you want to interpret. Close friends, in conjunction, who add a spicy remark and had done frequent 'pirouettes' to be able to get sited. Their lovely chat, something purposeless, may be to avoid the poignancy of intended remarks about life and events.

SPIRITUALITY VS REALITY

Sometime we think of spirituality within some limits. Why? Maybe we associate it with excessive drinking as alcohols were called spirits from ancient times and it could confuse some people. In modern times, and also, in not so modern ones, it could include the use of dangerous substances.

That is unfortunate because enjoyment in itself doesn't need toxicity to prevail. Maybe the origin of the word spirit refers to the spark that unleashes the enjoyment to be expressed. However, the enjoyment could be contained inside, expressed or both, it is the greatest manifestation of our life in this world. "Il tempo ultimo, che sappiano essere il tempo dell'essenzialita, rende molto piu chiara la percezione della mia interiorita...". Cited from an Italian magazine, (Ref # 14), and I have quoted it because it reflects the importance of getting to know ourselves to get deep in our spirituality.

It could get to a point that we might confuse reality with wishful thinking especially if we are listening to high lifting music. What to do next? Enjoy the moment or try to come to our senses for what we should be doing in every occasion? I don't know what to say, this could be such an intimate moment and we all should know by now what to do best.

I dare to say, if you surely are trying to follow Jesus Christ, the great master, with His law of love, just acknowledge that the good of the moment comes from Him who always want to reward you and even when there is nothing much deserving of reward, He still wants to draw you to Him, to live a life, give yourself to the moment if the moment surely overtakes you, thanking the Lord

There is a space in every human being that escapes the contact of even the closest person, mother, father, siblings, spouse or children. That space can only be occupied by God. Rolando, (Ref # 15). Amen, I say, thanking God for all His provisions.

Life evolves into love

References:

1-Einstein, Albert, "Out of my Later Years".

2-Gothman & Hanson, The Interplay of Genes.

1a- Einstein, Albert, "Out of my Later Years".

3-Camila Torres, Librarian and Tourist.

4-El Amor, song by Jose Luis Perales.

5-Delgado, Jorge, Lecturer in History and Geography.

6-Shapiro, Daniel, Beethoven Masterworks, CD.

7-Gutierrez, Hamilton, Barry University Musical Coordinator and Choir Director.

8-Father Lopez, Juan Jesus, Archeologist.

9-The Golden Compass, movie.

10-Hendrick, Graham, Composer.

11-Gospel of John, 1,1.

12-Father Lopez, Juan Jesus, Lecturer and Bible Specialist.

13-Garcia, Axel, Keen Observer and Interpreter.

14-Il Messagio de la Santa Casa-- Loreto.

15-Blanco, Rolando, Spiritual Master.

Life evolves into love

www.ingramcontent.com/pod-product-compliance
Lightning Source LLC
Chambersburg PA
CBHW031422040426
42444CB00005B/680